YOU CHOOSE BOOKS

THE OREGON TRAIL

An Interactive History Adventure

by Matt Doeden

Consultant:
Malcolm J. Rohrbough, PhD
Professor Emeritus, Department of History
The University of Iowa

CAPSTONE PRESS
a capstone imprint

You Choose Books are published by Capstone Press,
1710 Roe Crest Drive, North Mankato, Minnesota 56003
www.capstonepub.com

Library of Congress Cataloging-in-Publication Data
Doeden, Matt.
    The Oregon Trail : an interactive history adventure / by Matt Doeden.
        pages cm.—(You choose: history)
    Includes bibliographical references and index.
    Summary: "Describes the journey on the Oregon Trail from three different
historical perspectives"—Provided by publisher.
    ISBN 978-1-4765-0254-0 (library binding)
    ISBN 978-1-4765-3607-1 (paperback)
1. Oregon National Historic Trail—Juvenile literature. 2. Overland journeys to the
Pacific—Juvenile literature. 3. Frontier and pioneer life—West (U.S.)—Juvenile
literature. 4. Pioneers—West (U.S.)—History—19th century—Juvenile literature.
I. Title.
    F597.D66 2014
    978'.02—dc23   2013007022

Editorial Credits
Adrian Vigliano, editor; Bobbie Nuytten, designer; Wanda Winch, media researcher;
Charmaine Whitman, production specialist

Photo Credits
AP Images/North Wind Picture Archives, 12, 35, 67, 74, 88, 95; Capstone, 9;
Courtesy of L. Tom Perry Special Collections, Harold B. Lee Library, Brigham
Young University, 26; Courtesy Scotts Bluff National Monument, William Henry
Jackson Collection, 11, 23, 53, 58, 97, 105; Getty Images/DEA Picture Library, 73;
Library of Congress: Prints and Photographs Division/William Henry Jackson, 18;
North Wind Picture Archives, 44; Shutterstock: Sally Scott, 102, spirit of america,
50; SuperStock Inc.: Huntington Library, 63, 81, Image Asset Management Ltd.,
cover, SuperStock, 6

Printed in the United States of America in Stevens Point, Wisconsin.
052014   008259R

TABLE OF CONTENTS

ABOUT YOUR ADVENTURE

YOU are living in the United States in the mid-1800s—the time of the Oregon Trail.

In this book you'll explore how the choices people made meant the difference between life and death. The events you'll experience happened to real people.

Chapter One sets the scene. Then you choose which path to read. Follow the directions at the bottom of each page. The choices you make will change your outcome. After you finish your path, go back and read the others for new perspectives and more adventures.

YOU CHOOSE the path you take through history.

Wagon trains crossed the plains, heading west on the Oregon Trail.

On the
Oregon Trail

The mid-1800s were a time of expansion and exploration for the United States. Americans spread out across North America. The promise of a new life called to many. They claimed land for farming and raising livestock.

By the 1840s thousands of people were packing their belongings into wagons and heading west. Most followed the 2,000-mile Oregon Trail—a trip that took most settlers five or six months to complete. Long wagon trains rumbled across the plains of present-day Kansas, Nebraska, Wyoming, Idaho, and Oregon. Other trails branched off from the Oregon Trail. They led to California, Utah, and other places.

Turn the page.

While some people headed west looking for land, others rushed to California to search for gold. On January 24, 1848, James Marshall discovered gold at the sawmill he built for John Sutter on the bank of the South Fork American River near Coloma, California. Stories of the gold brought thousands of people to California who hoped to strike it rich for themselves.

Life was hard on the Oregon Trail. Much of the trail cut through the grasslands of the Great Plains. Settlers were far from civilization. Diseases such as cholera and smallpox were deadly. Floods, storms, and droughts threatened travelers and their animals. River crossings were dangerous. And while many American Indian groups left the travelers alone, others were less welcoming. Some Indians stole settlers' animals. Others attacked or killed the travelers because they felt threatened.

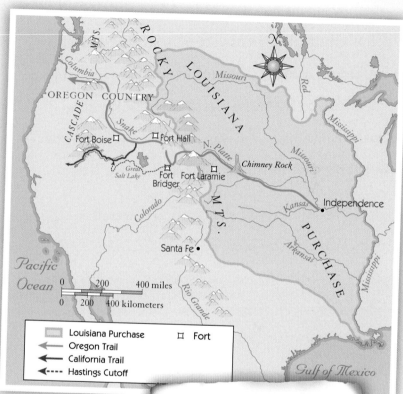

The Louisiana Purchase of 1803 doubled the size of the United States and opened the West for expansion.

Turn the page.

The dangers didn't stop the settlers, though. Most left from Independence, Missouri. They followed the trail across the plains. They passed landmarks such as Chimney Rock, Fort Laramie, Fort Bridger, Soda Springs, Fort Boise, and the Snake River along the way. Those who made it to Oregon found fertile land for the taking.

Could you survive the perils of the trail to make a new, better life?

Wagon trains lost many people to the dangers of the Oregon Trail.

To brave the Oregon Trail with a young family, turn to page **13**.

To guide a wagon train along the trail, turn to page **45**.

To head for California during the gold rush, turn to page **75**.

Life on the Oregon Trail could be especially hard for families with young children.

CHAPTER 2

Alone on the Plains

It started out as a great adventure. You were traveling west on the Oregon Trail with your parents, twin brother, and little sister. After years of struggling to get by in Missouri, your parents decided your family would start a new life out west.

But the adventure had turned into a nightmare. It started when your father got very sick. Your mother soon followed. It was smallpox. The others in your wagon train couldn't afford to stop. They didn't want to risk catching the disease, and they also needed to reach Oregon before winter.

13

Turn the page.

You decided to stop your wagon on the plains of Nebraska and watched as the train continued west without you. You did all you could to nurse your parents back to health. But your mother died five days ago. Your father followed yesterday. You buried them both along the trail and marked their grave with a cross made of sticks. Now the three of you are alone.

"We have to turn around," says 10-year-old Annabelle, her face streaked with tears.

Your brother, Lucas, sits with his head in his hands. Your father's rifle lies beside him. "There's nowhere for us to go back to," he says with a sigh. "We sold everything we own."

"But it's so far," Annabelle says. "How can we do it alone?"

You wipe your hands on your apron. "Lucas is right," you tell her. "Lucas and I are 17. We'll be 18 by the time we make it to Oregon. That's old enough to stake a claim and start a life."

"We have to go now," Lucas says. He stands and begins to hitch your mules to the wagon. "We're already almost two weeks behind the wagon train. We haven't seen another wagon for days. If we don't go now, we won't make it before winter."

Turn the page.

There's another reason to hurry. When you left Missouri, you thought you had enough food and supplies. You have a good team of mules to pull your wagon, as well as your father's reliable mare. You have pots, tools, fishing gear, and two good rifles. You left with water casks, flour, bacon, dried beef, sugar, and salt. But over time, your food stores have dwindled. You ate too much early in your journey and lost some food to spoilage. Even if you leave now, you're not sure you'll have enough.

Annabelle looks worried. "Look," you tell her. "We just have to follow the trail, right along the Platte River. We'll be to Fort Bridger before you know it."

The trail isn't hard to follow. The prairie grasses are beaten down to bare dirt in places. But that also creates a problem. Your mules need grass to eat. So does the mare. There isn't enough on the trail. Lucas suggests turning to the north in search of better grazing land. But you worry about leaving the main trail.

❖ To go in search of grazing land, turn to page **18**.

❖ To stay on the main trail, turn to page **20**.

Shoshone Indians were the dominant tribe along parts of the Oregon Trail.

It takes half the day, but you find the grass that the mules and horse need. You unhitch the team and let them graze. While they eat, you fix a light meal of bread and bacon. Lucas takes the rifle and heads off in search of game.

As your supper cooks, you hear the sound of approaching horses. But it's not Lucas. You gasp as you peer around the wagon and see three Indians riding toward you. Every settler on the Oregon Trail has heard frightening stories about Indians. Will they attack? Will they steal your supplies? You wish Lucas were here.

"Get in the wagon!" you shout at Annabelle.

You look at the back of the wagon. Your other rifle sits in there. Lucas keeps it loaded, and you know how to shoot it. But you have no idea how to reload.

➤ To greet the Indians and hope they are friendly, turn to page **21**.

➤ To shoot at the approaching Indians, turn to page **39**.

"We don't have the time," you say. "Maybe we'll find better grazing ahead. Let's stay on the trail."

Hours later, the trail is still mostly dirt and mud. The mules and the horse eat what grass you find. But you can already see the animals growing weaker and thinner. Without the mules, you'll be stranded.

The next day, you reach a small river. There's a spot where you can tell wagons have forded.

"Should we cross here?" you ask.

"I don't like the look of that current," Lucas says. "We don't want to get washed away. What if we turn north and look for a better crossing?"

"This may be the best crossing," Annabelle says. "Let's just go."

Both of them turn to you.

➤ To search for a better place to cross, turn to page 24.

➤ To cross here, turn to page 34.

The idea of firing at these Indians is stupid. You don't know that they're unfriendly. And if they are, one shot isn't likely to scare them away. You take a deep breath and step around to the front of the wagon.

"Hello!" you shout.

The Indians stop about 50 feet from the wagon. They approach carefully. You see rifles strapped to their backs, but they make no move for the weapons.

What appears to be the oldest Indian gets off his horse. He holds his hands out in front of him as he walks up to you. He walks past you, sticking his head inside the wagon. Does he mean to rob you?

Turn the page.

Annabelle rushes out, frightened. A few moments later, the Indian follows. He holds your spare rifle. He shouts something to one of the other Indians. The other man dismounts and pulls something from a saddlebag. It's a huge bundle of dried meat—buffalo, you guess. The eldest Indian gestures at the meat, then at the gun. He wants to trade!

You don't want to part with the gun. But you need meat, and you don't feel like you're in a very good place to negotiate. So you nod your head and take the meat. The elder Indian smiles, your rifle in his hands, and mounts his horse. Within a few minutes, they're gone.

Lucas comes back from hunting empty-handed. Annabelle excitedly tells him about your encounter.

"Well, at least it was the old rifle. It never shot straight anyway," Lucas says. "There must be 20 pounds of dried buffalo here. We'll be glad to have it. I guess it could have gone a lot worse."

Most Indians did not bother pioneers traveling through their lands.

→ *Turn to page 25.*

Crossing a rushing river with strong animals is dangerous enough. There's no way you're going to try it with tired, hungry mules. Lucas turns the wagon north.

It's the right decision. A few hours later you find a wide, shallow spot with little current. And even better, the banks are green with prairie grasses. You make camp and let the animals graze. Lucas and Annabelle go fishing and bring back half a dozen trout. Your animals aren't the only ones who will eat well tonight!

The next morning, you cross the river. The mules pull the wagon across without any trouble. Annabelle sings as you turn south and get back on the Oregon Trail.

You smile as the wagon rumbles over the rough trail. The days are long and hard. But you're making progress. You reach Fort Bridger. It's just a small trading post. But it's good to see other people. The trail has been getting lonely. Lucas spends what little money you have on food. You're loading up your wagon and getting ready to head out as an old fur trader approaches.

"Hello there," he says. "My name's George. Late to be headin' out on the trail."

Lucas nods. "We know. But we are making good time. Mules are much faster than oxen."

"Party came through a few months back," says George. "Headed to California. They said they were taking the Hastings Cutoff to make better time. Headed out southwest of here."

Turn the page.

Lucas smiles, shakes George's hand, and thanks him for the tip. "What do you think?" he asks.

Time is becoming a problem. But do you dare change routes now?

Fort Bridger was small, but it was one of the Oregon Trail's most important outfitting posts.

➤ *To stay on the Oregon Trail, go to page 27.*

➤ *To take the Hastings Cutoff, turn to page 37.*

"I think we should stick to the Oregon Trail," you say. Lucas agrees. You've come this far. You're not changing course now.

As you travel west, you notice more trees. As the days grow shorter, the flat ground gives way to hills and deep valleys. The grazing is better for the animals. They're regaining strength. It's fall when you reach Fort Boise near the Snake River. It's not a military fort, but it reminds you of one. Annabelle marvels at the fort's big brick walls.

At the fort a young, dark-skinned man helps you with your animals. He smiles at Annabelle and introduces himself as Kai. Then the fort's owner, Francois Payette, greets you. "Late in the year to be getting wagons through here," he says. "Haven't seen others in more than a week."

Turn the page.

"Is he an Indian?" Annabelle blurts out, pointing at the young man tending your animals.

Before you can shush her, Payette laughs. "No. He's from the Sandwich Islands. Some folks call them Hawaii. Most of my workers are from the islands. I find that they're good workers and easy to get along with."

"Do you have Indian trouble here?" Lucas asks, glancing back toward the stockades.

"Oh, the Shoshone don't cause too much trouble," Payette says. He speaks only to Lucas, ignoring you and Annabelle. "But they're not exactly friendly either."

"Best to be safe," Payette continues. "Speaking of which, it's awfully late in the year to be heading back onto the trail. You don't want to get caught in the first snows. You look like a strong lad. Can I interest you in wintering here? I'll put you to work in exchange for a roof over your head and food on your table. We can find some work for the girls as well."

You can tell Lucas thinks it's a good idea. But you're itching to find your new home.

➤ *To keep going, turn to page* **30**.

➤ *To winter at Fort Boise, turn to page* **31**.

"We've come so far," you say. "I can't imagine stopping now."

Lucas trades some of your remaining ammunition for food. Then you hitch up the mules and head back out onto the trail.

Less than a week later, the wind begins to howl out of the north. A flurry of snowflakes turns into a full-blown blizzard. You can't go anywhere in this weather. Lucas builds a fire to keep you warm. But you still shiver through the night.

It's another day before you can move again. The trail is wet and slick. You barely seem to be moving.

"We should turn around!" says Annabelle. "Mr. Payette will keep us safe through winter."

You look at Lucas. You can tell he agrees.

➤ To turn around and return to Fort Boise, turn to page 32.

➤ To keep going, turn to page 33.

Your shoulders slump in disappointment as you agree. Waiting until spring to move again seems like torture. But you have Annabelle's safety to consider.

It proves to be a smart decision. The year's first snowstorm hits only days after you arrive. You're glad you're not out on the trail in the snow and wind. Annabelle makes friends with Kai and several younger Hawaiian workers at the fort. Sleeping in the same spot every night is nice for a change.

➤ *Turn to page* **42**.

You don't have a choice. It's too late in the year to be on the trail. It's time to go back.

Kai greets you as you return. His smile tells you that he always expected you to come back. Payette's offer still stands. The three of you will spend the winter in Fort Boise. It's not what you wanted. But it's better than being trapped out there in the snow. And in time you come to enjoy your stay at the fort.

→*Turn to page 42.*

"I'm not going back," you say with a scowl.

Lucas sighs, but he doesn't argue. Your progress is slow. The days grow colder. Annabelle develops a terrible cough. You have no medicine. All you can do is try to keep her warm. But even that is difficult.

After weeks of travel, you reach a lush valley inside Oregon Country. Lucas is ready to stop. "There's good land right here," he argues. "We don't have to go all the way to Oregon City. We need to claim a spot and get started on a shelter for the winter."

➤ To make your home here, turn to page **41**.

➤ To continue on to Oregon City, turn to page **43**.

"There's no guarantee that there's a better spot," you decide. "We'll try to cross here."

There's a lot to do. If the river was shallow, the mules would just pull the wagon across. But that won't work. The animals will have to swim. Your wagon is built to float. All the seams are covered in wax.

You unhitch the mules from the wagon at the riverbank. Lucas takes the wheels off the wagon. It's not a perfect solution. Water seeps in slowly. But you'll be on the river only a few minutes. Nothing should get too wet.

The animals swim across as you launch the wagon and begin to float. Lucas uses a long stick to push the wagon along. But by the middle of the river, he has no control. The strong current is pulling you downstream.

The Snake River was generally considered the most dangerous crossing on the Oregon Trail.

"The mules!" shouts Annabelle. You turn and see the animals struggling. They're not strong enough to fight the current. One of them goes under. Seconds later, the other follows. You can't see the horse.

Turn the page.

Lucas frantically tries to guide the wagon to the shore. Boom! The wagon smashes into a rock. Water gushes through a large crack in the wood.

You grab Annabelle and dive toward the shore. The cold water takes your breath away. But you swim for all you're worth. Exhausted, you grab hold of a rock on the opposite bank. It's slick and you can't pull yourself up. But you are able to give Annabelle the boost she needs to climb out of the rushing river. You lose your grip and feel yourself being pulled back under the water. You can't see Lucas and don't know if he made it out of the water.

Annabelle is alive, at least. What her future holds, you can't guess. Your last wish is that she will find someone kind to look after her.

THE END

To follow another path, turn to page 11.
To read the conclusion, turn to page 103.

"Why not?" you say. "Let's do it!"

Lucas turns the wagon southwest. The route takes you over high mountain passes. They're difficult to navigate, but the dips in the mountains are the only places you can hope to cross. Lucas guides the wagon along rough trails and through steep canyons. The sure-footed mules handle the terrain well.

You make it over the mountains and start crossing the Great Salt Lake Desert. Your water reserves get lower. A few days later one of your mules collapses and dies. You try to hitch the horse to the wagon. But the animal won't pull. Even if it did, the other mule refuses to pull without its partner.

Turn the page.

"What are we going to do?" asks Annabelle.

You wish you had an answer. You're alone on the desert, stranded. You'll be out of water in days, with no relief in sight.

"I think we made a mistake," says Lucas.

That's an understatement. All you can do is wait and hope help comes along. But as you gaze over the dry plains, you know that there is no real hope. All three of you will pay for your bad decision with your lives.

THE END

To follow another path, turn to page 11.
To read the conclusion, turn to page 103.

You have to defend yourself! You grab the rifle. The three Indians are almost to the wagon. One raises an arm. Could he have a gun?

No time to find out. You level the barrel and pull the trigger. Crack! The force of the shot half spins you around. You look up. The three Indians have stopped. One dismounts. He puts his hands in front of him, a gesture meant to calm you. The other two remain on horseback. Both carry rifles. But the guns are not aimed at you. You realize that the Indians never meant you harm. You fired on innocent men.

The Indian approaches you. Calmly, he takes the gun from your hand. He shakes his head. Then he turns to leave.

Turn the page.

Another crack sounds across the plains. The Indian crumples to the ground. It's Lucas! You can only imagine what he thought when he saw the Indians at your wagon, taking the rifle from you.

"No! Stop!" you shout, but it's too late. The other two Indians have already raised their weapons. One shot catches Lucas in the arm. The other slams into his chest. He falls from his horse.

Two men are dead already. As the Indians ride toward you, rage in their eyes, you know you'll soon be dead too. You just hope they spare little Annabelle.

THE END

To follow another path, turn to page 11.
To read the conclusion, turn to page 103.

Lucas is right. You'd always imagined riding triumphantly into Oregon City. But that's not the way it's going to happen. Annabelle is very sick. You need to get her to a real shelter before it gets even colder. Surviving this winter is going to be very difficult.

"I agree," you say. Who cares whether you get to Oregon City? This trip was about getting a new home, and you've found one. Now it's time for the real work to begin.

THE END

To follow another path, turn to page 11.
To read the conclusion, turn to page 103.

By spring you're eager to get going. Once the trail is clear and dry, you pack your belongings. Payette loads you up with supplies, and your animals are well fed and strong. Annabelle wishes Kai good-bye, and you're back on the trail.

The land here is green and lush. You're passing small farms. Children run out to wave as you pass. You know you've arrived in Oregon Country. The going is easy all the way to Oregon City. You find a plot of land several miles from the city and stake your claim. There's still a lot of work to do. But you can't wait to get started on your new home and new life.

THE END

To follow another path, turn to page 11.
To read the conclusion, turn to page 103.

"We set out for Oregon City, and that's where we're going," you insist.

After an hour of arguing, you finally get your way. Lucas is angry and doesn't speak to you for the rest of the day.

Two days later, snow falls so hard that you have to stop. The wind howls and the temperature drops. A tree branch falls and rips the top of your wagon. It's a cold, miserable night. In the morning, you realize that Annabelle is too quiet. You break down in sobs as you realize she didn't survive the night. As the weather continues to rage, you understand what a horrible mistake you've made. Even if you somehow survive, you'll never forgive yourself.

43

THE END

To follow another path, turn to page 11.
To read the conclusion, turn to page 103.

Leading a wagon train on the Oregon Trail required skill and knowledge.

CHAPTER 3

LEADING THE WAY

On horseback, you look out over several dozen wagons. Settlers are bustling around them. The people are headed west in search of a new life. They've hired you to be their guide.

Life is changing out here in the west. Years ago you were part of a busy fur trade. But the demand for furs has all but disappeared. Like many other "mountain men," you find yourself in need of work.

You know the country well. You've survived out here all your life. But are you ready to lead others and be their captain?

Turn the page.

You lead your group of wagons west out of Independence, Missouri. The travelers are excited. Children run alongside the wagons. Husbands and wives sit proudly, driving their teams of mules, oxen, and workhorses.

A young man approaches you. He introduces himself as John. "I served a while in the army," he explains. "If you need a steady rifle along the way, I'm your man. I can pick off an Indian from a hundred yards."

You nod, trying not to roll your eyes. The man may be a good shot. But if he thinks that your group would survive a standoff with hostile Indians, he's a fool. You've heard the stories about Indian attacks. But you've lived on the frontier your whole life. You've dealt with many of the native people along the trail. Indian attacks are not high on your list of worries.

As the days and miles pass, the enthusiasm of the group dips. The sun is hot and the trail is hard. Then come the rains. It pours for days at a time. The trail becomes a muddy mess. It's no trouble for your horse. But the wagons can barely move.

One dreary morning, you hear it. Snap! One of the wagons breaks an axle. The wheel comes off and cracks in half. Some families carry a spare wheel. But not this one. And no one is eager to give up a spare.

The wagon belongs to a young couple, Jeb and Martha. You're their guide. But you're not responsible for maintaining their wagon. They have a horse. You could order them to ride back to Independence on their own. Or you could ask another family to take them on.

➤ To leave the couple, turn to page **48**.

➤ To ask another family to take them on, turn to page **52**.

The Oregon Trail is hard enough without taking on extra people. You hate to do it, but your responsibility is to the other emigrants in your wagon train.

"I'm sorry," you tell Jeb and Martha. They looked shocked and panicked as they realize what you're about to say.

"Please, no," begs Martha.

"You have a horse. Ride back to Independence. With no wagon to pull, you can be there in less than a week. We're moving on. I'm sorry."

"Don't leave us alone out here," they plead. But your mind is made up. Before long they're nothing more than specks on the distant horizon. You notice that none of the other travelers talk to you the rest of the day. Well, that's fine by you.

The journey goes smoothly over the next week. You cut northwest across Nebraska until you meet the big Missouri River. You travel alongside it. The weather is good, and the animals have ample room to graze.

Before long you have a friend. Will, a 12-year-old boy traveling with his family, is constantly at your side. You tell him stories of the old days, when the Oregon Trail was for fur traders like yourself. One day you're telling him a story when he suddenly shouts, "Look at that!"

Far in the distance, you see Chimney Rock towering above the horizon. "That," you tell Will, "is Chimney Rock. It's a sign telling us that we're almost out of the plains. We'll soon be in mountain country."

Turn the page.

Chimney Rock is near Bayard in western Nebraska.

Excited, Will dashes off to tell his fellow emigrants. As he leaves, John approaches. "We have a problem," he explains. "Several people are sick. They're vomiting and have terrible diarrhea. I think it's cholera."

You shake your head. Cholera is one of the most dreaded diseases on the Oregon Trail. It can lead to a long, painful death. "Why wasn't I told earlier?"

"Nobody wanted to say anything," John answers. "After you left Jeb and Martha behind, people worried. What are we going to do?"

→ To make camp and treat the sick, turn to page 54.

→ To continue on with hopes of leaving the sick at a fort, turn to page 55.

You sigh. You can't just leave them here. "Can anyone take them?" you ask.

You're lucky. John volunteers. "I have room in my wagon. Load up what you can," he tells the couple. "Let's keep moving."

By afternoon, you're back on the move, one wagon short. A few days later, a young boy shouts from atop his family's wagon. "Buffalo!" He's right. A huge herd grazes in the distance.

John rides alongside you on his mare. "What do you think? Should we get us a buffalo?"

In the 1800s pioneers nearly hunted the buffalo to extinction.

You know he's excited at the prospect of a hunt. But hunting buffalo is dangerous. They are big, powerful beasts. And a gunshot could cause the herd to stampede. If they headed toward the wagons, it could be a disaster.

➺ To go hunting, turn to page **56**.

➺ To play it safe and leave the herd alone, turn to page **59**.

You have no choice. Your party is as good as dead if you keep going with so many sick people.

The healthy members of your party help the sick ones. A nearby stream provides fresh water, and you make sure the sick get plenty to drink. "Cholera is a disease of the gut," you explain to Will. "We need to flush it out with water."

It takes a week before everyone is well enough to move again. The stop puts you behind schedule, but everyone survives. That's what's important.

54

→ *Turn to page* **62**.

"We can't stop here," you explain. "Fort Laramie is a few days ride. We'll get medical help there."

Your luck doesn't get any better over the next several days. Strong thunderstorms dump rain down on you. Every small stream becomes a rushing river. You have to take your time crossing. But your people are getting sicker and sicker. You're about a day out of Fort Laramie when the first person dies. Two more die before you reach the fort.

You don't find much more help there. Nobody wants to allow the sick inside the fort. They're afraid of an outbreak.

"We could strike out," suggests one man, Marcus, whose family has escaped the disease. "Leave the sick here. Some of us still have a chance. Let's take it."

➤ To leave the sick at the fort and return to the trail, turn to page 71.

➤ To stay with the main group, turn to page 72.

Four of you head out hunting. You and John lead the way. James and Abraham, a father and his teenage son, follow.

The herd is massive. It stretches out across the prairie. The buffalo are so thick that the landscape looks black in places.

"Careful now," you whisper as you approach the herd. The four of you crawl up a small rise on the prairie, keeping yourselves hidden. You load your rifles. All three of you take aim at a large cow on the fringe of the herd.

Before you can fire, something spooks the herd. A sound like thunder rises up as it starts to move. James and Abraham turn to rush back to the wagons. You shout out a warning and grab for John. But he's already aiming. Bang! His rifle shot rings out over the sound of the herd. The cow lurches and falls to the ground.

The herd is on the move. But you're in luck. They're running away from the sound—and away from the wagons. A few minutes later, they're far in the distance. You and John go to claim his kill. You butcher the meat and bring the best cuts back to the wagons. The women will prepare some of it right away. They will dry the rest. Your food problems are solved.

Turn the page.

A buffalo stampede could damage wagons and injure or kill pack animals or pioneers.

You slowly make your way across the plains. In time, you pass Chimney Rock, a major landmark on your trail. You're about to leave the plains and enter mountain country.

➻ *Turn to page 62.*

The thought of the meat a buffalo would provide is tempting. But you don't want to take the risk. "We'll keep moving," you say. "I don't want to be caught in the middle of a stampede."

You can see the disappointment in John's eyes, but he doesn't question your judgment. You swing wide around the great herd and continue on your way.

The little wagon train continues on the trail, moving along the Missouri River. The land has few trees, so you collect buffalo chips to fuel your fires. Twelve-year-old Will laughs at the idea of burning buffalo droppings, but you have few other options.

Turn the page.

Trouble begins as you move out of the prairie into mountain land. Fire consumes much of the food in one wagon. A barrel of flour becomes soaked and ruined. The others share their food, but as supplies grow low, tensions rise. Within a week, only a handful of settlers have much food left at all. You're still days away from Fort Laramie.

"We can't continue to feed everyone," says a man named Charles. "I fear for my family's safety. There are five families with enough food for the trip. We want to continue on alone. Are you with us?"

➤ To go with the small group that has enough food, go to page **61**.

➤ To stay with the main group, turn to page **69**.

You were hired to lead people to Oregon. But they're not paying you enough to die out here. You'll stick with the group that has the best chance of making it to Oregon.

"We can't tell anyone about our plan," you say. "Desperate men might choose to fight."

Early the next morning, the five wagons begin to move before the others know what's happening. You half expect them to chase you. But they don't seem to have the energy. And so you're back on the trail. You now have a much better chance to make it to your destination.

61

Turn to page 71.

You're behind schedule, so you push hard into the mountain country. Heavy rains have swollen the region's many rivers. Ferries help the settlers cross the biggest ones, such as the Snake River. But the smaller rivers present a problem. They are running deeper and faster than usual, and there are no ferries to help you cross.

Late one afternoon your group approaches such a river. You know it from your fur trading days. It's normally just a few feet deep. But now it rushes along, wider and deeper than you've ever seen it.

"Can we cross here?" asks Will. "It's going to be dark soon. We'd better get started now."

He's right. You'd like to scout the river a bit before bringing your people across. But the sun is getting low in the sky. And you notice dark clouds in the west. Maybe it would be better to cross before more rain can fall and make the river deeper still.

Over the years, ferries were built at some river crossings along the Oregon Trail.

→ To cross now, turn to page **64**.

→ To scout the river and make camp here, turn to page **66**.

"Looks like more rain tonight," you say. "I think we'd better cross now. I know this river. It shouldn't be too deep, even now."

You'll float the wagons across. Everyone knows what to do by this time. One by one, they move their wagons to the edge of the river. They remove their wheels and unhitch their teams of mules and oxen, so the animals can swim across on their own. The wagons aren't watertight, but they're close enough for this short trip.

You lead the way. Your horse, a tall stallion, has done this a hundred times. He doesn't shy away as you guide him into the water. The water comes up to the stallion's neck, but no deeper. You emerge safely on the other side and help the others safely up the steep bank.

"We did it!" shouts Will.

A few weeks later you enter Oregon Country. "So much land, with nobody living on it!" says John. You shake your head. There's no point reminding him that people have been living here for thousands of years. It's a time for celebration, not argument. You've successfully guided your party to Oregon. Your days of fur trading may be over. But your life as a guide along the Oregon Trail has just begun.

65

THE END

To follow another path, turn to page 11.
To read the conclusion, turn to page 103.

You think you know this river, but you've never crossed when it was this high. "We'd better make camp," you say. "I'll scout the river and see if we can cross here."

As the settlers make camp, you lead your horse into the river. It's deep, but not too deep. You should be able to make it across.

But that night a storm brings heavy rain. When you wake, everything is drenched. The emigrants are cold and miserable. But you tell them the good news—you can cross here.

You lead the way on the back of your trusty stallion. But as you near the middle, you realize that the current is much stronger than it was last night. And the water is deeper.

In an instant, the powerful current sweeps your horse off its feet. You struggle to keep your head above the freezing water. You hear screams behind you, but there's nothing you can do to help anyone.

A wagon train races to cross a stream to escape a fire.

Turn the page.

Frantically, you try to swim toward shore.
But the current is too strong. Your clothes are
drenched, and the weight is pulling you under.
You fight with all the energy you have, but it's not
enough. Your head slips beneath the churning
surface. You didn't account for all that rainfall
rushing down the riverbed. It's a mistake that has
cost you your life.

68

THE END

To follow another path, turn to page 11.
To read the conclusion, turn to page 103.

"These people are relying on me," you tell the man. "I'm not going to abandon them."

You try to convince the families with the food to stay, but they refuse. You can only watch as they ride off into the distance.

"We'll be all right," you assure the others. But John gives you a look that says he doesn't believe it. Neither do you.

You and half a dozen wagons slowly move across the prairie toward Fort Laramie. But soon hunger and disease set in. Your people are at their weakest when cholera begins to spread through the camp.

Turn the page.

You're only a day from Fort Laramie when the disease strikes you. You feel as if your guts have been turned inside out. A handful of healthy settlers strike out ahead, promising to bring back help. But you know how deadly cholera can be. Help won't return in time for you. Your journey ends here. You just hope some of the others manage to survive the dangerous Oregon Trail.

THE END

To follow another path, turn to page 11.
To read the conclusion, turn to page 103.

The rest of the trip goes smoothly. It seems you've left your bad luck behind you—along with some of the people you were hired to guide. But you refuse to dwell on that.

Your small group arrives in Oregon. Fertile land stretches in every direction, most of it available for the taking. But you won't be claiming any. You're no farmer. You realize with a hint of sadness that you're not much of a guide either.

THE END

To follow another path, turn to page 11.
To read the conclusion, turn to page 103.

"I've made some mistakes along the way," you explain. "But not this time. We'll stick together."

You get supplies from the fort and make a camp a few miles along the trail. Two more people die, but the others recover. The somber group heads back out onto the trail.

Even Will seems to have lost his excitement. As you finally approach Oregon City, you feel a sense of relief that it's almost over.

"What will you do now?" asks John.

"I don't know," you answer. "I don't think I made much of a guide."

"We had some bad luck," John offers. He knows that you made some mistakes, but you can tell that he respects you for sticking with the main group.

Many pioneers arrived in Oregon City to claim land and start their new lives.

You're surprised to find that this respect means a lot to you. Maybe you didn't do so badly, after all. Still, you can't stop thinking about the people you lost along the way. Could you have saved them if you had made better choices?

THE END

To follow another path, turn to page 11.
To read the conclusion, turn to page 103.

A large wagon needed at least six oxen to pull it. A smaller wagon could manage with fewer.

CHAPTER 4

On the
California Trail

"There's a fortune out there," says the old man with a toothless smile. You smile back, happy to have someone to talk to. It's the summer of 1849 and you're on your way to California. There's gold there. Like thousands of others, you're hoping to get your share.

The old man, Samuel, rides with you as you follow the Oregon Trail. You're arriving at Fort Hall in eastern Oregon Country. It's near the place where the California Trail splits off from the Oregon Trail. Samuel is riding a horse, with only a few saddlebags for supplies. You are driving a team of oxen pulling a covered wagon. The wagon is stocked with supplies, from food and water to mining equipment. Oxen are slow but reliable.

Turn the page.

"Trade those beasts for a horse at Fort Hall," suggests Samuel. "The gold won't last forever. We'll be there in a month by horseback. Take you three times that long with this wagon."

It's tempting. You've driven this team of oxen all the way from your family farm in Kansas. They've done well so far, following the Oregon Trail. They've taken you through storms, floods, across rivers, and even around a herd of buffalo. But they'll be even slower in mountain country.

"I'm not sure," you say. "Taking the wagon is slower, but it's also safer."

"Nobody ever got rich by playing it safe. I'm riding ahead to the fort. I'll be there in a few days. You find me if you want to ride together."

You munch on some dried apples and carrots as you watch him ride off. You carefully steer your wagon along deep ruts in the trail. Many have come this way before, and the ground is scarred with their tracks.

➤ To continue with your wagon and supplies, turn to page **78**.

➤ To sell off your oxen, wagon, and supplies and travel by horseback, turn to page **80**.

You'd love to be in California sooner. But you feel safe in the wagon. You're not ready to give that up. When you finally arrive at Fort Hall, you tell Samuel good-bye. "Maybe I'll see you in California," you say. He laughs and assures you that by the time you reach California, he'll already be rich.

You set out from Fort Hall along the Snake River. The Oregon and California trails split where the Raft River meets the Snake. The emigrants headed for Oregon continue west, while you turn south.

The trail takes you deep into the Rocky Mountains. The going is slow. As you approach a mountain pass, the trail narrows to barely more than the width of your wagon. Rain falls as you approach a steep, narrow section of the trail. You're not sure your oxen can handle the slick rock. But it's cold, wet, and the air is thin. Stopping here isn't going to make you or your animals any stronger. And you don't know how long the rain will last.

→ To continue up the slick trail, turn to page **83**.

→ To pull aside and wait for the rain to pass, turn to page **93**.

As you inch along, you make your decision. Samuel is right. You'll be on the trail for another couple of months at this rate. What if all the good claims are gone? It's time to move.

Samuel rides out to meet you as you approach Fort Hall. You're in luck. There's a family on their way to Oregon. Their team of mules has died. They need something to pull their wagon. The family pays you well for your oxen. You use the money to buy a sturdy mare you call Daisy. You load up saddlebags with food and supplies, selling your wagon and the rest at a fraction of their true value.

"Don't you worry," Samuel says. "When you strike gold, you won't even remember what they were really worth."

And so the two of you head out together. Just west of the fort, the Oregon Trail and the California Trail split. You turn south, heading deeper into mountain country. Daisy is sure-footed. You and Samuel make good time, passing several groups of wagons along the way. You're glad to have the old-timer's company.

Fort Hall was originally built as a fur trading post.

Turn the page.

You climb higher, headed for Granite Pass. You see the City of Rocks, a group of tall rock formations. It's nothing like your home in Kansas. Samuel is an expert hunter, and most nights you roast fresh meat over a fire. You're not a big fan of jackrabbit meat, but with your limited supplies, you can't be fussy.

A few days later, you spot a camp ahead. You see a few tents and some horses. "Should we stop and say hello?" asks Samuel.

It's always nice to see new faces and exchange information. But out here, you never know whom you can trust. You might be safer just moving along.

→ *To steer clear of the camp, turn to page 86.*

→ *To stop at the camp, turn to page 98.*

You can't stop every time a little rain falls. The rain could continue for days. The oxen are warm and in a rhythm. You'll keep going.

You hold your breath as the trail narrows. A sharp drop lies just feet from the trail. One misstep and you'll be dead. But your sturdy oxen are well trained. They plod along, pulling the wagon over the bumpy trail.

In a few hours the worst is over. You made it! With the mountain pass behind you, you're headed back downhill. There are a few more parts of the trail that make you nervous, but you manage without any trouble.

Turn the page.

The days pass as you slowly move along the banks of the Humboldt River. You approach the part of the trail known as the Forty Mile Desert. You're stocked with supplies, including lots of water. That's a good thing, because the desert is brutally hot. You try to travel at night, when it's cooler, and sleep during the day.

Near the end of your desert journey, you spot another wagon. A man and woman are waving their arms at you from atop it. They look like fellow emigrants. But you can't be sure.

→ To see if the people need help, go to page **85**.

→ To avoid them, turn to page **88**.

"Hello!" you shout as you approach the couple. Thomas and Annie are newly married and headed west to look for gold. But they didn't bring enough water into the desert, and their mules died of thirst. Now their wagon is stranded. They're very glad to see you.

"We're almost out of water," says Annie. "Can you help us? We don't have much to offer you, but we do have some information on a good spot to pan for gold. We'll be happy to share it with you."

Your supplies are stretched thin, and you're not sure about taking on strangers. But this is an adventure, and out here, everyone is a stranger to you.

➤ To give them a bit of water and leave them, turn to page **89**.

➤ To take them with you, turn to page **91**.

"I don't like it," you tell Samuel. "There are no wagons. They don't look like emigrants. Let's not risk it."

Samuel gives the camp a hard look and nods. "You're right. Not everyone out here is friendly. Let's keep moving."

The two of you continue over the mountain country. You cross Granite Pass and make a careful descent. You come to the Humboldt River. You follow it west to the deep Carlin Canyon, where you must ford the Humboldt several times. Then you're facing the toughest part of your trip—the Forty Mile Desert.

"There'll be little food and no water after this point for a stretch," Samuel warns. The desert is a graveyard for unprepared emigrants. Your supplies are running low and you're eager to cross the desert.

Samuel suggests camping here for a few days so you and your horses can rest before the long journey.

↠ *To get some rest, turn to page* **96**.

↠ *To keep going, turn to page* **100**.

The California Trail split into more than five different routes through the Sierra Nevada.

You've heard tales about thieves on the California Trail. There's no way to be sure these people aren't out to steal everything you own. It's not worth the risk. You steer wide of the wagon and continue on by yourself.

But you wonder if you made the right decision. What if they were just emigrants like you? Have you doomed them by not stopping to help?

You feel a bit lonely as you ride off. What will happen to those poor people stuck in the desert? You made it because you were well prepared. But what if you'd hit some bad luck? You'd sure like someone to stop and help you.

You sigh and shrug. What's done is done. You're getting close to your destination. You and your team of oxen just keep plodding westward. You cross the Sierra Nevada. These mountains seem almost small compared to the Rockies. Within a week, you're in California, making your way toward the American River. This is near where James Marshall and John Sutter discovered gold a year and a half ago. You don't know much about panning for gold. All you can do is pick a spot and get started.

Turn the page.

Like many 49ers, as those rushing to California are called, you spend little time setting up a home. You live out of your wagon and spend your days sifting through river silt. But your efforts are not rewarded. You find a few flakes of gold, but not nearly enough to make a living. One day you decide it's time to call it quits. You came out here to make your fortune. You realize now that you'll be lucky just to find a job somewhere and make a living.

THE END

To follow another path, turn to page 11.
To read the conclusion, turn to page 103.

"Of course I'll take you," you tell the couple. Thomas rushes up to shake your hand. Annie gives you a hug. They grab what few supplies they have from their wagon before you leave.

You have to admit that it's nice to have company. Annie tells you that her brother, Ben, has been to California. He's told them of a perfect spot for panning for gold. The three of you travel west over the Sierra Nevada and into California. Thomas leads the way as you search for a small tributary of the American River. It's not too far from where John Sutter discovered gold a year and a half before. It takes a long time to find the spot, but you finally do. The three of you claim spots next to each other and get to work.

Turn the page.

Your luck is better than you could ever have imagined. Within a week you've made more by selling your gold than you would have made in a year in Kansas. Most of the 49ers who rushed to California meet with little success. But for a few, including you, the gold rush will make you rich beyond your wildest dreams.

THE END

To follow another path, turn to page 11.
To read the conclusion, turn to page 103.

You don't want to risk the slick trail. If your oxen slipped, you'd be as good as dead. So instead, you pull your wagon over along a wider stretch of trail and wait for better conditions.

As you start a fire, you realize how thin the air is up in the mountains. Even a little effort has you gasping for breath. You're cold and wet, and there's little to burn up here. It's a long, cold night. There's nothing for your oxen to graze on this high up. You feed them out of your meager store of grain.

Turn the page.

The next day is even colder and wetter. You're miserable. It doesn't seem like the rain will ever stop. You realize stopping here was a big mistake. You hitch up your team, but the animals are sluggish. One of them loses its footing on the slick rock. The wagon doesn't go down, but the animal's leg is broken. There's nothing you can do for it. Up here, an ox with a broken leg is dead. You have no choice but to get your rifle and put it out of its misery.

The wagon is too heavy for one ox to pull. Now you're stranded in the mountains. You're cold, your supplies are limited, and you have no way to get your wagon back down. There's only one choice—pack up supplies and hike back the way you came.

The death of an ox could create a dangerous situation for a wagon train.

You hope to find help along the way back. Or maybe you'll become a victim of the dangerous California Trail. Either way, your journey has been a failure.

THE END

To follow another path, turn to page 11.
To read the conclusion, turn to page 103.

You spend the next day and a half at the headwaters of the Humboldt. You and your horses feel stronger. The next evening you're ready to start again. Samuel says that many emigrants start the crossing in the evening. It's a good idea. The ride is cool and brisk. Doing this in the afternoon heat would sap the animals' strength much more quickly.

Your preparation pays off. It's a long, tiring crossing, but you make it to the Carson River. There you find the precious water that you all need. From there, it's on to your final obstacle. The Sierra Nevada mountain crossing is almost easy compared to your crossings of the Rocky Mountains and the Forty Mile Desert.

"We did it," says Samuel as the two of you descend. "Now we just need to find a spot, stake our claim, and get rich!"

You smile at your friend. "Well, let's get to it."

It is estimated that at least 25,000 pioneers traveled on the California Trail in 1849.

THE END

To follow another path, turn to page 11.
To read the conclusion, turn to page 103.

You approach the camp on horseback. "Hello!" Samuel shouts. A man comes out from one of the tents. He's carrying a rifle. Out of the corner of your eye, you spot two more men perched on a rock outcropping to your right. A quick glance shows two more to your left.

"I don't like this," you whisper.

"Why don't you two just get down off those fine horses, real slow," says the man. He has weathered skin, a thick beard, and cold eyes.

"Horse thieves," Samuel whispers back. You want to turn and flee, but you know the other men have you in their sights.

"Don't do nothing crazy now," says the man. "We don't want to kill you. We just want your horses."

In a flash, Samuel pulls a revolver from his pack. He raises it toward the man's head. BOOM! A gunshot rings out. Samuel slumps in his saddle and falls to the ground, dead. The horse thief turns his gaze to you. "Well, how about you?"

Shaking, you climb down from your horse. You reach for your saddlebags, but the man stops you. "Leave that too. Sorry, boy. Can't spare anything for you. Now turn and march."

You do as you are told. As you run away, you realize your terrible situation. Samuel is dead. With no horse and no supplies, you're as good as dead as well.

THE END

To follow another path, turn to page 11.
To read the conclusion, turn to page 103.

"I feel fine," you say. "The horses seem strong. Let's continue."

Samuel suggests waiting until night to make the crossing, but you don't agree. How would you see where you're going? "We'll get a start, camp for the night, and ride out in the morning," you reason. Samuel shrugs, but does not argue.

At first you make good time. But as the sun rises in the sky, the temperature soars. You're going through what little water you have much more quickly than you'd planned. Samuel gives some of his water to his horse. But you don't have any to spare.

Daisy isn't doing well. She's thirsty. Her pace slows. Before long she stops moving and hangs her head to the ground. The sun is starting to set, but the day's heat has done its damage. You ask Samuel for water, but he sadly shakes his head.

"Your horse is done. Mine can't carry us both. If I give you water, we're all good as dead. I don't intend to die in this desert. Good luck to you, son."

And with that, your friend rides off to the west. You drop to the ground, realizing your mistake. Hundreds of people bound for California have died here. That total will soon rise by one.

THE END

To follow another path, turn to page 11.
To read the conclusion, turn to page 103.

Wagon ruts dug into the stone are still visible along the Oregon Trail.

CHAPTER 5

Life After the Trail

The Oregon Trail changed the face of North America. Historians have estimated that during the peak of emigration, about 350,000 people followed the Oregon, California, and Mormon trails west. An estimated 20,000 of them died along the way.

Before the 1840s the West had been largely an unknown frontier. Most of the Europeans in the area were British and American fur traders. But as hundreds of thousands of settlers flocked west, all that changed. The population of California soared. Towns sprang up all over the state. Many of them quickly grew into cities. California became a state in 1850.

103

Meanwhile, Oregon was growing as well. Farms thrived there. Its population grew, and Oregon became a state in 1859. The American West was slowly being settled by pioneers.

The wave of emigration wasn't good for everyone, however. The American Indians of the West paid a high price. Many were driven from their lands. Christian missionaries came west to convert native tribes to Christianity. For many tribes, their entire way of life was wiped out within a generation or two.

In time the Oregon Trail became obsolete. In 1869 the transcontinental railroad was completed. It connected the two North American coasts. Travel by covered wagon was no longer necessary. The days of the Oregon Trail were over.

Evidence of the Oregon Trail still exists today. In places, the land remains scarred by deep wagon ruts. Gravestones still stand along the trail. And names and initials carved or painted onto rocks in places such as the City of Rocks in Idaho can still be seen. Even more than 150 years after the peak of travel on the trail, these artifacts remind us of the long and dangerous journey so many took in search of a better life.

Pioneers could get land from the U.S. government if they agreed to clear and farm it.

Timeline

1803—The United States doubles in size when it buys 530 million acres of land from France.

1812–1813—Fur trader Robert Stuart and his party become the first white people to travel the Oregon Trail; their journey began in Oregon and ended in St. Louis, Missouri.

1836—The first wagon train leaves Independence, Missouri; the trail at that time extends to Fort Hall, Idaho.

1843—A train of about 1,000 emigrants travels the trail to Oregon.

1846

A group of Mormons, who belonged to the Church of Jesus Christ of Latter-day Saints, leaves Illinois and travels the trail to Utah; this establishes the Mormon Trail, which branched off from the Oregon Trail near Fort Bridger, Wyoming.

The 87-member Donner Party becomes trapped in the Sierra Nevada mountains of California in November; 39 members die during the winter from starvation and disease.

1848—James Marshall discovers gold near the mill he built for John Sutter in California.

1849

A cholera epidemic begins on the trail, killing thousands of emigrants.

Gold-seekers called 49ers rush to California, increasing the state's population from about 15,000 to 100,000.

1855–1857—American Indian wars occur in the West; fear of war keeps emigrant travel on the trail to about 5,000 settlers.

1858—Gold is discovered in Colorado, sparking about 10,000 people to travel there in search of fortune.

1869—The completion of the transcontinental railroad ends much of the travel on the Oregon Trail, but it is still used until the 1880s.

OTHER PATHS TO EXPLORE

In this book you've seen how the events surrounding the Oregon Trail look different from several points of view.

Perspectives on history are as varied as the people who lived it. You can explore other paths on your own to learn more about what happened. Seeing history from many points of view is an important part of understanding it.

+ Many people of the Mormon faith traveled along the Oregon Trail and Mormon Trail to Utah. What motivated them to make the journey? How did their journeys differ from the journeys of other explorers? (Key Ideas and Details)

+ Suppose you were a Native American living along the Oregon Trail. Describe how you might have felt about the settlers passing through your land. What might you be curious about? What might worry you? Use details from the text to support your answer. (Integration of Knowledge and Ideas)

+ The U.S. Army operated forts along the Oregon Trail. What challenges did these soldiers face? Do you think those forts were necessary? Explain why or why not. (Integration of Knowledge and Ideas)

READ MORE

Domnauer, Teresa. *Westward Expansion*. New York: Children's Press, 2010.

Friedman, Mel. *The Oregon Trail*. New York: Children's Press, 2013.

Lassieur, Allison. *Westward Expansion: An Interactive History Adventure*. Mankato, Minn.: Capstone Press, 2008.

McNeese, Tim. *The Oregon Trail: Pathway to the West*. New York: Chelsea House Publishers, 2009.

Musolf, Nell. *The Split History of Western Expansion in the United States*. North Mankato, Minn.: Compass Point Books, 2013.

INTERNET SITES

Use FactHound to find Internet sites related to this book. All of the sites on FactHound have been researched by our staff.

Here's all you do:
Visit *www.facthound.com*
Type in this code: 9781476502540

Glossary

cholera (KOL-ur-uh)—a dangerous disease that causes severe sickness and diarrhea; cholera is caused by contaminated food or water

emigrant (E-mi-gruhnt)—a person who leaves his or her home to settle in a new country or land

ford (FORD)—to cross a river

mare (MAIR)—an adult female horse

ration (RASH-uhn)—a fixed amount of something, such as food or water

rifle (RYE-fuhl)—a long-barreled gun that is fired from the shoulder

smallpox (SMAWL-poks)—a disease that spreads from person to person, causing chills, fever, and pimples that scar

stallion (STAL-yuhn)—an adult male horse

BIBLIOGRAPHY

Brands, H.W. *The Age of Gold: The California Gold Rush and the New American Dream.* New York: Doubleday, 2002.

Dary, David. *The Oregon Trail: An American Saga.* New York: Alfred A. Knopf, 2004.

Klausmeyer, David. *Oregon Trail Stories: True Accounts of Life in a Covered Wagon.* Guilford, Conn.: TwoDot, 2004.

McLynn, Frank. *Wagons West: The Epic Story of America's Overland Trails.* New York: Grove Press, 2002.

Peavy, Linda, and Ursula Smith. *Pioneer Women: The Lives of Women on the Frontier.* Norman: University of Oklahoma Press, 1998.

Rau, Weldon W. *Surviving the Oregon Trail, 1852.* Pullman: Washington State University Press, 2001.

INDEX